THE
GRAND CHAM'S DIAMOND

A Play in One Act

by

ALLAN MONKHOUSE

LONDON
SAMUEL FRENCH LIMITED

SAMUEL FRENCH LTD
26 SOUTHAMPTON STREET, STRAND, LONDON, W.C.2

SAMUEL FRENCH INC.
25 WEST 45TH STREET, NEW YORK, U.S.A.
7623 SUNSET BOULEVARD, HOLLYWOOD 46, CAL.

SAMUEL FRENCH (CANADA) LTD
27 GRENVILLE STREET, TORONTO

SAMUEL FRENCH (AUSTRALIA) PTY LTD
159 FORBES STREET, SYDNEY

MADE AND PRINTED IN GREAT BRITAIN BY
LATIMER, TREND AND CO. LTD, PLYMOUTH

MADE IN ENGLAND

THE GRAND CHAM'S DIAMOND

Presented by John Drinkwater at the Birmingham Repertory Theatre, on 21st September 1918, with the following cast of characters:

(in order of their appearance)

MRS PERKINS	*Cathleen Orford*
MR PERKINS	*Reginald Gatty*
MISS PERKINS	*Sidney Leon*
A MAN IN BLACK	*Noel Shammon*
ALBERT WATKINS	*J. Adrian Byrne*

The action of the play passes in a sitting-room in a small house in a London suburb

THE GRAND CHAM'S DIAMOND

SCENE—*A sitting-room in a small house in a London suburb. Some time after the evening meal.*

The window is in the R *wall, and the door is* L *of the back wall. The mantelpiece is in the* L *wall. The furniture is ordinary; there is a table* C *with three chairs to it, a sofa at an angle down* RC, *armchairs above and below the fireplace, and a sideboard up* R. *On the mantelpiece* L *is a clock. Other furniture as the producer desires. Ornaments, ashtrays, etc., are scattered round the room. The room is lit by electric-candle wall-brackets.*

When the CURTAIN *rises,* MR PERKINS *is sitting in the armchair below the fireplace reading a newspaper.* MRS PERKINS *is sitting in the armchair above the fireplace darning a sock, and* MISS PERKINS *is at the table* C *engaged on a jigsaw puzzle.*

MRS PERKINS. What I mean t' say is that it's not much fun for us.

MR PERKINS. All right, Ma.

MISS PERKINS (*engaged on her puzzle*) It makes a long evenin' of it. Same every night. We 'ave our tea and then we just set down till it's time to go to bed. It's not fair.

MR PERKINS. Same for all of us.

MRS PERKINS. That it's not.

MR PERKINS. Why isn't it?

MRS PERKINS. Do y' or do y' not go out o' this 'ouse every mornin' and spend the day out?

MR PERKINS. It'd be a poor job for you if I didn't.

MRS PERKINS. I don't say anythin' about that. I don't interfere.

MR PERKINS. 'Ow could y' interfere?

MISS PERKINS. Bother!

MRS PERKINS. Don't intterup' like that when me and your pa's talkin', Polly.

MISS PERKINS. My name isn't Polly.

MR PERKINS. What is it?

MISS PERKINS. It's Marie.

MR PERKINS. Well, I'm blowed!

MRS PERKINS. An' why shouldn't she 'ave a bit of a change? She's tired of bein' Polly.

MISS PERKINS. I do think we might have a little more change.

MR PERKINS. Don't you start.

MISS PERKINS. We might have gone out to the pictures tonight, as mother said.

MR PERKINS. Your young man might 'ave come and found you out.

MISS PERKINS. You know he's engaged in the evenings.

MR PERKINS. Yes, and what at?

MISS PERKINS (*loftily*) Never mind!

MRS PERKINS (*still darning*) I do think Polly, that he ought to be a bit more open with you. What *does* he do?

MR PERKINS (*putting down his paper*) Ay; what does Albert Watkins do?

MISS PERKINS. Never you mind!

MRS PERKINS. 'E's never told 'er.

MR PERKINS. I 'ope it's nothin' to be ashamed of.

MISS PERKINS. P'raps I know more than you think.

MRS PERKINS. 'As 'e said?

MISS PERKINS. It's confidential. (*She returns to her puzzle*)

MR PERKINS. Oh, I know that tale!

MRS PERKINS. Well, Polly's got 'er young man, and you've got your business an' out all day seein' people. What 'ave I got?

MR PERKINS (*indignantly*) Well, what should y' 'ave? What does any woman 'ave? I dunno what you're botherin' about. Y' 'ad a week at Margate this year.

MRS PERKINS (*derisively*) 'Ome from 'ome!

MR PERKINS. A good woman ought to like 'er 'ome.

MRS PERKINS. I never said I didn't like it.

MR PERKINS. Well . . .

MRS PERKINS. 'Ome's a place to come back to.

MISS PERKINS (*looking up from her puzzle*) Mother's romantic. That's what she is. (*She returns to her puzzle*)

MRS PERKINS. What *is* that, Polly? It's a word I never rightly . . .

MR PERKINS (*disgustedly*) Romantic! At 'er age!

MRS PERKINS. You know what it is, do y'?

MR PERKINS. It's penny dreadfuls, and the pictures, and gassin' about love and the deep blue sea.

MRS PERKINS. Well, y' might do worse.

MR PERKINS. Whatever's come over 'er? (*He picks up his paper*)

MRS PERKINS (*putting down her darning*) I've always thought I should like to travel.

MISS PERKINS (*at her puzzle*) I think there's a bit missing.

MRS PERKINS. Eh? A bit missin'? That's the way with me; there's always bin a bit missin'.

MR PERKINS (*throwing down his newspaper*) I dunno why y're startin' like this now. Y've 'ad all these years to settle down in. What's come over yer?

MRS PERKINS. Eh! Don't ask me. I think 'er Albert's comin' about 'as unsettled me.

MISS PERKINS (*looking up*) Albert!

MRS PERKINS. Well, I see 'im an' you, and I think what might 'a' been.

MR PERKINS. What's that? (*He stands up, collects his pipe from the mantelpiece, then sits, fills his pipe and lights up during the next few lines*)

MRS PERKINS. Well, I was young onct.

MR PERKINS. But y're not now.

MRS PERKINS. You've no call to throw it in m' teeth.

MR PERKINS. Teeth indeed!

MRS PERKINS. Don't be insultin', Mr Perkins.

MR PERKINS. I wasn't bein'.

MRS PERKINS. Yes, y' was.

MISS PERKINS. I don't see why Albert should unsettle you.

MRS PERKINS. If I was you I'd want to know 'ow 'e spends 'is evenings.

MISS PERKINS. It's no business of yours, Ma.

MR PERKINS. It'll be some business of mine. I think it's about time Albert spoke to me.

MISS PERKINS. Spoke to you?

MR PERKINS. Placed 'is position an' prospects before me.

MISS PERKINS. Well, I believe he's a confidential agent.

MRS PERKINS. A what!

MR PERKINS. What sort of a agent?

MISS PERKINS. It's confidential—or financial, p'raps.

MR PERKINS. He's kiddin' yer.

MRS PERKINS. Do they work at night?

MISS PERKINS. I've always understood that Rothschilds and people like that did this business at parties—on the quiet.

MR PERKINS. Bosh!

MISS PERKINS. Oh, very well, Pa.

(MISS PERKINS *settles to her puzzle.* MRS PERKINS *darns solidly.* MR PERKINS *returns to the paper. There is a short pause*)

MRS PERKINS. Well, it's too late for the movies now.

MISS PERKINS (*finding the missing piece of the puzzle*) Ah! that's it.

MRS PERKINS. What's in the paper, Pa?

MR PERKINS. There's a Cabinet crisis.

MRS PERKINS. Isn't there anythin' interestin'?

MR PERKINS. 'Ere's a child stole a shillin', an' swallowed it t' escape detection.

MRS PERKINS. Pore thing!

MR PERKINS. 'Ere! Is this more in your line? Great Jewel Robbery! The Grand Cham's Diamond Missing.

MRS PERKINS. Eh! What's that?

MISS PERKINS. Who is the Grand Cham? (*Tired of her puzzle, she stands up and wanders down* R *to the sofa, where she sits*)

MR PERKINS. 'E's—one o' them Eastern potentates. 'E's been stayin' at the *Majestic Hotel*. The diamond was taken out of the settin' and a walnut substituted.

MRS PERKINS. A walnut! It must be a whopper.

Miss Perkins. Why did they substitute a walnut?

Mr Perkins. You must substitute somethin'.

Miss Perkins. Why?

Mr Perkins. I don't know. They always do. The brightest treasure of the East. Not the slightest trace. Supposed Asiatic gang. Sherlock Holmes and Father Brown have been summoned, and a telegram dispatched to Mossier Lecock.

Mrs Perkins (*with satisafaction*) Well, that's somethin' like.

Miss Perkins. What's it worth?

Mr Perkins. Eh! I dunno. Thousands, thousands. They say it makes the Koh-i-noor take a back seat.

Mrs Perkins. Reely?

Mr Perkins. What 'ud you do, old lady, if I brought it 'ome for y'r birthday?

Mrs Perkins. Well, I'd wear it, I suppose.

Miss Perkins. You'd never dare, Ma.

Mrs Perkins. I would that.

Miss Perkins. But thieves'd always be after it.

Mrs Perkins. What'd these thieves do with it when they've got it?

Mr Perkins. I s'pose they'd chop it up and sell it in bits.

Mrs Perkins. What a shame!

Mr Perkins. I dessay they're off to South America.

Mrs Perkins. Why?

Mr Perkins. No extrydition.

Mrs Perkins. What's that? D' y' mean last 'dition extra?

Miss Perkins. No, Ma. It means that thieves can't be turned out.

Mrs Perkins. Why not?

Mr Perkins. It's like it used to be with slaves here. Once the South American flag's waved over 'em, they're all right.

Miss Perkins. It isn't all one country there, Pa.

Mr Perkins. Well, I reckon they're much of a muchness.

Mrs Perkins. An' could you sell it there?

MR PERKINS. Yes, they're great people for jewel'ry.

MRS PERKINS. Polly, you're doin' nothin'. Y' might as well be mendin' that blind.

(MR PERKINS *returns to his paper, then gradually nods off*)

MISS PERKINS. Oh, bother!

MRS PERKINS. It looks bad hangin' down like that.

MISS PERKINS (*rising and going to the window*) People'll see in.

MRS PERKINS. There's not many passin' at this time o' night.

MISS PERKINS (*taking the blind down*) It makes it so public. (*She crosses* L) Where's the white thread, Ma?

MRS PERKINS (*handing her needle and thread*) Here y' are. Now, make a job of it.

(MISS PERKINS *takes the needle and thread, crosses* R *and sits on the sofa.* MRS PERKINS *darns and yawns.* MR PERKINS *snores gently*)

Might as well all be asleep.

MISS PERKINS. Listen, Ma!

MRS PERKINS. Somebody runnin'. Seem in an 'urry.

(*Something crashes through the window and falls on the floor amid a shower of broken glass*)

MISS PERKINS. Good gracious! (*She jumps up*)

MRS PERKINS. Mercy on us!

MR PERKINS (*waking up with a start*) Fire! Where is it?

MRS PERKINS. Nonsense, Pa! It's them boys. Out arter them.

MR PERKINS (*jumping up*) What! Where?

MISS PERKINS. No. Don't go. Don't leave us. It can't be boys.

MR PERKINS (*seeing the broken window*) This is very careless, Polly.

MISS PERKINS. It wasn't me. It's a stone, I think.

MRS PERKINS. They're far enough now. Where is it?

MISS PERKINS. I'm all of a tremble.

MRS PERKINS. You ought to 'ave run right out, Pa, and you might 'ave caught 'em. I never did see such a thing.

MR PERKINS. It's an outrage, this is. Did y' see anybody?

MRS PERKINS. We 'eard somebody runnin'.

MISS PERKINS. I thought I 'eard somebody passing after that. Quietly like. Runnin' very light.

MR PERKINS. Nonsense, Polly. Better put that blind up now.

MISS PERKINS. You put it up.

MR PERKINS. Do as I tell you.

MISS PERKINS. I don't like.

MRS PERKINS (*rising*) 'Ere, 'ere. Give it me. (*She takes the blind from Polly and puts it up at the window, then peers out into the street*)

MISS PERKINS. Come away, Ma.

MR PERKINS. Where's the stone?

(*They all look about the floor*)

MISS PERKINS. Here it is. Here's something. (*She picks it up*) Why, it's a lump of glass!

MR PERKINS. Let's look!

MRS PERKINS. Let me see.

(*They crowd round*)

MR PERKINS. I say!

MISS PERKINS. What is it? What is it?

MRS PERKINS. Give it me, Polly. (*She grabs it*)

MR PERKINS. Hold it up to the light.

MISS PERKINS. Why? What can it be?

MRS PERKINS (*relinquishing it to her husband*) Nonsense! Nonsense! (*She goes back to her chair and begins to fumble with her darning. She is greatly agitated*)

MR PERKINS. It's a rum thing, this is.

MISS PERKINS. Eh! Isn't it beautiful?

MR PERKINS. It might be a . . .

MISS PERKINS. Diamond?

MR PERKINS. Nonsense!

MRS PERKINS (*rushing forward*) Hide it! (*She seizes the diamond and looks about the room*)

MISS PERKINS. Why! What d' y' mean, Ma?

MRS PERKINS. It's it.

MR PERKINS (*feebly*) What's it?

MRS PERKINS. You know.

MR PERKINS. What—what—what rubbish! The idea!

MRS PERKINS (*looking at it in her palm*) It's the Grand Cham's diamond.

MR PERKINS. Then it's dangerous.

MRS PERKINS. Never mind that.

MISS PERKINS. What shall we do? (*She begins to whimper*)

MRS PERKINS. Stop that, Polly.

MR PERKINS. P'raps we'd better look out for a policeman.

MRS PERKINS. No.

MR PERKINS. If it is it we're not safe.

MRS PERKINS. I don't care.

MR PERKINS. But what d' y' want to do?

MRS PERKINS. Here! Let's put it inside the clock. (*She moves to the mantelpiece, opens the back of the clock and crams it in*) Now!

MR PERKINS. What are y' up to, Ma?

MISS PERKINS. I wish you'd throw it out in the street again.

MRS PERKINS. No, no.

MR PERKINS. But what *are* y' up to?

MRS PERKINS. It's come to us, this 'as. We'll stick to it if we can.

MR PERKINS. But . . .

MISS PERKINS. Oh, Ma!

MRS PERKINS. They may not find the 'ouse again. They're all alike in this street.

MR PERKINS. There's the broken window.

MRS PERKINS. Let's 'ave the bits of glass out. Then it won't be noticed. (*She crosses to the window, and peers out into the street. Then she begins to pluck the fragments of broken glass from the window. She winces and licks her finger*)

MR PERKINS. You've cut yourself now.

MRS PERKINS. Never mind that. Polly, pick all the bits off the floor. Don't leave a trace. (*She licks her finger*)

(POLLY *picks up the bits of glass from the floor*)

MR PERKINS. Now, what's all this about?

MISS PERKINS (*on the floor*) I dunno what's come over 'er.

MRS PERKINS. 'Ere, Polly, look alive. 'Ave y' got 'em all?

MISS PERKINS. All I can find.

MRS PERKINS (*peering out of the window*) Drat it! A bit's fallen outside. Go out and pick it up, Pa. No; p'raps better not.

MR PERKINS. Look here! What's y'r game?

MRS PERKINS. Give here! (*She takes all the fragments together and puts them under the sofa cushion. She looks round the room, listens at the window, then returns to her chair, sits and takes up her darning*) If anyone comes, mind, we know nothin' about it.

MR PERKINS. It depends 'oo comes, doesn't it?

MRS PERKINS. No.

MR PERKINS. It might be the police.

MRS PERKINS. Never mind the police.

MR PERKINS. Why! What d' y' mean? What *do* y' mean?

MRS PERKINS. It's the chanct of a lifetime. We'll take it.

MISS PERKINS. Oh, Ma! (*She moves down* R *and sits nervously on the sofa*)

MR PERKINS. Look 'ere . . .

MRS PERKINS. It's come to us. It might 'a' bin the answer to a prayer.

MR PERKINS. Was it?

MRS PERKINS. Not exactly, but I've been thinkin' a lot.

MR PERKINS. More likely the devil.

MRS PERKINS. There's no such thing. Y're talkin' nonsense.

MR PERKINS. It's awful talk, this.

MISS PERKINS. Why! What could you do with it?

MRS PERKINS. Chop it up and sell it.

MR PERKINS. Where?

MRS PERKINS. In South America.

MR PERKINS. Good 'eavens!

MISS PERKINS. Ma, how can you?

MR PERKINS. 'Ave y' took leave of y'r senses?

MRS PERKINS. Yes, if y' like.

MR PERKINS. Well, I've 'eard tell as women aren't honest like man, and now I know it.

MRS PERKINS. 'Ow do I know you're honest?

MR PERKINS. I've never took a thing in my life. I've a record, 'aven't I?

MRS PERKINS. I dessay. I dunno. I won't give it up. I won't. I won't. So there!

MR PERKINS. 'Ow can y' 'elp it?

MRS PERKINS. I've sat there darnin' and mendin', waitin' and dozin' till I'm tired. I've never 'ad a go at anythin'. The chanct 'as come.

MISS PERKINS. I did think you were honest, Ma.

MRS PERKINS. Honest! It's ours.

MR PERKINS. 'Ow can it be?

MRS PERKINS. 'Oo's is it?

MR PERKINS. Why! That Grand Cham's.

MRS PERKINS. An' 'ow did 'e get it? 'E's a tyrant. 'E stole it off some nigger. Now it's come to me. It's mine. It's mine as much as anyone's. It's come like a miracle.

MISS PERKINS. But you can't keep it.

MR PERKINS. Y'r ma amazes me. (*Very bewildered, he sits slowly on the chair above the table*)

MRS PERKINS. First thing in the mornin' y'll get a list o' them ships sailin' for South America.

MISS PERKINS. Oh, Ma! Ma!

MR PERKINS. She's off 'er chump.

MRS PERKINS. I'll go alone if y' like.

MR PERKINS. It's dangerous. It's dangerous. There may be a revolver levelled at y' now. (*He looks round nervously*)

MRS PERKINS. I don't care.

MR PERKINS (*to Miss Perkins*) I never knew she was like this.

MISS PERKINS. South America? Where?

MRS PERKINS. Y' shall 'ave jewels and dresses no end, Polly.

MISS PERKINS. Don't, Ma.

MR PERKINS. South America! Like that chap Jabez Balfour.

MISS PERKINS. He was brought back, wasn't he?

MR PERKINS. I object to be put along of 'im, any'ow.

MRS PERKINS. We'd manage better than that. Riches! Livin' at ease. Motors an' champagne. We've never 'ad a chanct!

MR PERKINS. It can't be done. It's all nonsense. An' it's 'orrible to think of.

MRS PERKINS. Oh! It's a beautiful thing. I couldn't bear to break it up. We'll keep it. We'll look at it now and then. Every Sunday.

MR PERKINS. Sunday!

MRS PERKINS. I could go on settin' 'ere if I knew it was there all the time. I think I could be 'appy.

MISS PERKINS. You'd never be safe.

MRS PERKINS. Safe! I've bin too safe.

MR PERKINS. Oh, missis! Oh, missis! (*He rises and walks around agitatedly*)

MISS PERKINS. It's strange nobody's come.

MRS PERKINS. Nobody's comin'. It's a gift.

MR PERKINS. It may not be—what y' think.

MRS PERKINS (*fiercely*) It is.

MR PERKINS. Then they'll be after us. Police—or worse.

MRS PERKINS. Let 'em come.

(*There is a ring at the door-bell. MR PERKINS stands stock-still. MISS PERKINS jumps up in alarm. MRS PERKINS stares straight ahead*)

MR PERKINS. Now, there.

MISS PERKINS. Oh, dear!

MRS PERKINS (*rising abruptly*) You'll not say a word. You'll do as I tell you. Mind that. We know nothing.

MISS PERKINS. There's the window.

MRS PERKINS. Leave that to me.

MR PERKINS. Oh! But, I say . . .

MRS PERKINS. Thomas Perkins, you'll rue it to your
dyin' day if . . .

(*The bell rings again*)

MR PERKINS. Who's goin'?
MRS PERKINS. I am. Remember!

(MRS PERKINS *goes out*)

MISS PERKINS. What are we to do, Pa?
MR PERKINS. Eh! I'm beat.
MISS PERKINS. Shall we throw it out of the window?
MR PERKINS. No, no. Best not. Humour her a bit. It
may be nothin'.
MRS PERKINS (*off*) No, you don't. 'Ere. I tell yer . . .
STRANGER (*off*) Excuse me.
MRS PERKINS (*off*) Pa, 'ere's a man forcin' 'is way . . .
MISS PERKINS. Oh, dear!
MR PERKINS. Dash it all! I say!

(MRS PERKINS *enters, followed closely by a dark*
STRANGER, *dressed in black. She is resisting his advance, but
he presses on ruthlessly. As the* STRANGER *enters,* MRS
PERKINS *gives way and changes her tactics*)

MRS PERKINS. Well, I must say! Pushin' a lady about
like that! What bis'ness 'ave y' 'ere?
STRANGER. I've told you, madam. (*He moves down* LC
a little)
MRS PERKINS. A fine tale! Y'r boy an' 'is glass marble!
Where is 'e? I tell yer we know nothin' about it. Do we,
Pa?

(*Behind the Stranger,* MRS PERKINS, *with a terrific frown,
shakes her fist at Mr Perkins.* MR PERKINS *moves down* C)

MR PERKINS (*feebly blustering*) Now what's all this?
MISS PERKINS. Oh, Ma!
MRS PERKINS. Shut up!
STRANGER. I'm sorry to intrude, sir, but I've lost
something in your room.
MRS PERKINS (*moving down* L) What nonsense! 'Ow
could yer?

STRANGER. As I have told this lady, my little boy . . .

MRS PERKINS. Where is 'e?

STRANGER (*to Mr Perkins*) His favourite glass marble. He pretended to throw it. It slipped from his hand and, I am sorry to say, went through your window. I apologize, and shall be glad to pay. Please give me the marble at once. Where is it? I've no time to lose.

MRS PERKINS. Where's the boy?

STRANGER. He's just round the corner.

MRS PERKINS. D' y' expect us to believe that tale?

STRANGER (*with a flash of menace*) You'd better. (*To Mr Perkins*) Now, sir!

MR PERKINS. It's a bit thick, y' know; I mean thin.

STRANGER. It will have to do. No trifling. Come! (*He looks round the room, having cursorily glanced at the floor. He strides to the window and pulls down the blind*)

MRS PERKINS. None o' y'r liberties here. Get out!

MR PERKINS. 'Ere, y' know! (*Aside to Mrs Perkins*) Ma, I don't like it.

STRANGER. The devil! Where's the glass?

MRS PERKINS. What glass?

STRANGER. The pane's gone. You see! I knew this was the house.

MRS PERKINS. That's easy explained.

MISS PERKINS. Oh, Ma! Tell him, and . . .

MRS PERKINS. Of course I'll tell 'im. (*She menaces Miss Perkins surreptitiously*) It's my daughter's new-fangled ideas of ventilation. She would 'ave it so. It's been that way a fortnight. No—let's see—today's Tuesday. Nigh on a month.

STRANGER. Damnation! Where is it? Where's the diamond?

MRS PERKINS (*with a shriek of exultation*) The dimond!

STRANGER. Yes, let me tell you then. Your lives are in danger. You have got the Grand Cham's diamond.

MR PERKINS. 'Ow did it get 'ere?

STRANGER. The thief was pursued. He threw it in.

MR PERKINS (*querulously*) Why did 'e throw it in 'ere?

STRANGER. Don't be a fool.

Mrs Perkins. An' 'oo are you?

Stranger. I am—the Grand Cham's representative.

Mrs Perkins. Prove it.

Stranger. Enough of this.

(*The* Stranger *draws a revolver.* Miss Perkins *shrieks and sinks down on the settee.* Mr Perkins *recoils and edges away.* Mrs Perkins *stands firm*)

Mr Perkins. Ma! Ma!

Stranger (*rapping the butt of the revolver on the table*) Where is it?

Mrs Perkins. I'll tell yer.

Stranger. At once.

Mrs Perkins. I've swallered it.

Stranger (*greatly discomposed*) What!

Mrs Perkins. It went down as easy as an oyster.

Stranger. Swallowed it! You're joking!

Mrs Perkins. No. I got the idea out of the evenin' paper. Where is it, Pa? (*She moves to the armchair below the fireplace*) 'Ere. (*She picks up the paper*) "Child swallows Shillin'. Curious Case."

Stranger (*to the others*) Is this true?

Miss Perkins. Oh, I don't know.

Mr Perkins. Y' see, I was asleep.

Stranger. Asleep!

Mr Perkins. Wasn't I, Mother?

Mrs Perkins. 'E'd sleep through anythin'.

Stranger. D' you mean to say . . . Where is it?

Mrs Perkins. I've just told yer.

Stranger. On your oath . . .

Mrs Perkins. Oath! D' y' doubt the word of a lady?

Stranger. Then—d' you feel it—I mean—whereabouts is it now?

Mrs Perkins. I don't think that's a question a gentleman 'd ask.

Stranger. Kites of hell! You'll have to be cut open.

Mrs Perkins. Nay, I won't.

Stranger (*to himself*) Cremation! Would it melt the diamond?

MRS PERKINS. I won't be cremated. There! Y've got to get the deceased's consent. I'm goin' to be buried when my time comes.

(*The* STRANGER *paces about in agitation, while* MRS PERKINS *controls the others by nods and winks*)

STRANGER. What's to be done? An emetic?

MRS PERKINS. You'd better go 'ome an' say it's lost.

STRANGER. Unhappy woman! Do you understand that your life is a trifle, a pawn in the game?

MRS PERKINS. Pawn! Yes, an' y' can't get it out without the ticket.

STRANGER. It's impossible. It can't be. (*He turns on the others*) The truth! Did she swallow it? If she did, she dies.

MISS PERKINS. Oh, no, no. She didn't. (*She rises*)

MRS PERKINS. You silly!

MISS PERKINS. Oh, Ma!

MR PERKINS. Ma, Ma, what can we do?

MRS PERKINS. Y' can 'old y'r tongues. Y're no 'elp at all.

STRANGER. What folly this is! What can you do with it? That diamond means death to you. Death! Destruction! You haven't a chance of keeping it. You're mad. Your lives now are not worth a minute's purchase.

MISS PERKINS. Give it up, Ma. I'll tell you where it is. It's . . .

MRS PERKINS (*in a terrible voice*) Stop!

MR PERKINS. What can you do, Ma? Chuck it! Chuck it!

MRS PERKINS. 'E don't bluff me. 'E's in a great 'urry. I believe 'e's the thief.

STRANGER. Thousand devils! We're wasting time. (*He looks at the clock and then plucks out his watch*) Your clock's slow. It's stopped. It was that time when I came in.

MISS PERKINS. Tell him. Tell him.

MR PERKINS. Oh, chuck it!

STRANGER (*perceiving that he is getting warm*) What stopped the clock?

MISS PERKINS (*hysterically*) Give it 'im. (*She collapses on to the sofa*)

MRS PERKINS. Polly, I'm ashamed of yer.

(*The face of* ALBERT *appears at the window, but they do not see it*)

STRANGER. Is it there?

(*He makes for the clock, but* MRS PERKINS *throws herself in front*)

MRS PERKINS. No, it's not; and y' shan't meddle with my furniture.

STRANGER (*pointing the revolver at her*) Move aside!

MRS PERKINS. Move aside yerself.

STRANGER (*hesitating, then turning the revolver on* MISS PERKINS) Is it there? Quick!

(MISS PERKINS *shrieks, a hand with a revolver in it is thrust through the empty pane, the revolver is fired, the* STRANGER *drops his, stamps, curses, and wrings his hands.*

ALBERT *opens the window-sash and springs into the room*)

MISS PERKINS. Albert!

MRS PERKINS. What! It's Albert.

(*The* STRANGER *rushes to the light switch and turns off the lights. Darkness, shouting and confusion.*

The lights go on. The furniture is disarranged, the STRANGER *and the clock have gone.* MISS PERKINS *is on the sofa,* MR PERKINS *is standing below the table,* MRS PERKINS *is seated above the fireplace, and* ALBERT *is by the door*)

ALBERT (*moving down* LC) Who's got it?

MR PERKINS. He's gone.

MISS PERKINS (*rising*) Oh! Albert!

ALBERT. Where's the diamond?

MR PERKINS. It was in the clock.

ALBERT. The clock? Where is it?

MISS PERKINS. Oh! Albert!

MR PERKINS. 'E's taken it. 'E's got the clock.

MRS PERKINS. Nay, 'e 'asn't. (*She produces the clock from under her petticoats*)

MR PERKINS. Well, I'm blowed! (*He sits* R *of the table*)

MISS PERKINS. Oh, Ma!

ALBERT. What is it? Have you got it?

MRS PERKINS. I've got it right enough. (*She rises, carries the clock to the mantelpiece, opens it, takes out the diamond, then puts the clock straight on the mantelpiece*) Will that gentleman come back?

ALBERT. No, he won't.

MRS PERKINS. How d' y' know?

ALBERT. I know.

MRS PERKINS. Polly, just put that blind back, will yer? I don't like bein' too public.

MISS PERKINS. Oh! I daren't.

ALBERT. Now, ma'am, give it to me.

MRS PERKINS. Eh?

ALBERT. Let's have it. Quick.

MRS PERKINS. Where d' you come in, Albert?

ALBERT. Come on. This'll be the making o' me.

MRS PERKINS. O' me, too, I 'ope. But 'adn't we all better be movin'?

MISS PERKINS. Where to, Ma?

MRS PERKINS. Out at the back door. Pack a few things in a bag.

ALBERT. What are y' up to? Wha' do' y' mean?

MRS PERKINS. Now, Albert, there's no time to make explanations. We're all in at this, aren't we?

ALBERT. Well—in a way. But look here . . .

MRS PERKINS. South America's the place, isn't it? D' y' know anythin' o' the sailin's? Or 'ad we better cross to France? Better take the midnight train somewhere.

ALBERT (*to the others*) Has she gone dotty?

MRS PERKINS. Y're all asleep. Come on, Polly. A few things in a bag. (*She crosses down* C) Now, Pa. Better put this light out p'raps. Is the front door shut? Look at the time-table, Pa.

(MRS PERKINS *goes to move up* L *of the table.* ALBERT *intercepts her*)

ALBERT. Give me the diamond. I dunno what y're talkin' about.

MRS PERKINS. Nay, I stick to this.

ALBERT. You can't! What nonsense! Give it here! This job's the makin' o' me. Let's have it.

MRS PERKINS. Nay, it's mine, an' I'll stick to it.

ALBERT. Yours?

MRS PERKINS. Yes, Dimonds like this belongs to them as can get 'em. Nobody's honest with things like this. I got it an' y' shall all share. But it's mine. It's mine. Eh! It's a beauty. I'd stick to this if all the p'lice in London was after me.

ALBERT. Y'd do what?

MRS PERKINS. Ay, an' Scotland Yard, too.

ALBERT. Bah! *I'm* Scotland Yard.

MRS PERKINS. What!

MISS PERKINS. Oh! Albert! (*She rises*)

ALBERT. Didn't y' know? Didn't y' guess? Didn't y' understand? What did y' take me for?

MRS PERKINS. D'y mean to say . . .

ALBERT. I mean t' say it's 'igh time I was on my way back with this diamond. The gang's all rounded up by this time.

MISS PERKINS. The gang?

MR PERKINS. That feller was one of 'em, then? Where is he?

ALBERT. He was copped when he left 'ere. Y' didn't know y'r 'ouse was surrounded.

MRS PERKINS. But 'ow did the dimond come 'ere? 'Oo threw it in?

ALBERT. I did.

MISS PERKINS. You!

MR PERKINS (*rising*) You did!

ALBERT. I did that.

MR PERKINS. Why?

ALBERT. Becos they were after me. I was a dead man if I stuck to it then. I threw it in 'ere to gain time and knowin' the 'ouse.

MISS PERKINS. Well, I never!

ALBERT. They're a desp'rate lot.

MR PERKINS. It's all most unusual. Never since I've been an 'ouse'older 'ave I . . .

MISS PERKINS. Oh, Albert! You might 'ave told me.

ALBERT. I 'ad my reasons.

MRS PERKINS. Y're a detective, then?

ALBERT. I am that. So let's 'ave it. I tell yer I must be off.

MRS PERKINS (*holding up the diamond, but away from him*) Look at it, Albert!

ALBERT. I see it.

MRS PERKINS. Can y' be honest? Look at it!

ALBERT. She's off 'er chump.

MR PERKINS. She doesn't reely mean it. I've borne a 'igh character all my life.

MRS PERKINS (*passionately*) It's *my* dimond.

MISS PERKINS. I'm ashamed of my ma.

MR PERKINS. My employers 'as always put the utmost confidence in me.

ALBERT. What's she up to? Now, ma'am, you'll just 'and that over or . . .

MRS PERKINS. Or?

ALBERT (*producing a whistle*) I wouldn't 'andle yer myself.

MRS PERKINS. That's it, is it?

ALBERT. That's it.

MRS PERKINS. Then let it go the way it came. (*She throws the diamond through the window with a crash of breaking glass*)

MR PERKINS. 'Old on. There's another pane gone!

ALBERT. Oh, 'elp!

(ALBERT *rushes out hurriedly*)

MISS PERKINS. You'll ruin us, Ma. (*She runs to the window*)

MRS PERKINS (*dusting one hand against the other*) A good shuttance. (*She moves L and sits above the fireplace*)

MISS PERKINS (*looking out of the window*) Oh! I hope he'll find it. There he is, and a policeman's with him. They've got it, I think. Yes. Albert! Albert! I wish he'd look up. They're seeing if it's damaged. There! He's waved his hand.

MRS PERKINS. Well, we've 'ad quite a busy evenin'.

MISS PERKINS. I don't know what Albert'll think of you.

MRS PERKINS. 'E's not going to marry me, thank 'eaven.

MR PERKINS (*moving* LC) D' y' want t' know what *I* think of yer?

MRS PERKINS. Go on! Y've no 'magernation.

MISS PERKINS. I never thought to be ashamed of my own mother.

MR PERKINS. Wantin' in the very el'ments of morality. I wonder 'ow sossiety'd get on if they was all like you.

MRS PERKINS. Polly, put up that blind. It's a bit chilly with them broken panes.

MISS PERKINS. Most unlady-like as well.

(MISS PERKINS *replaces the blind at the window, then returns to her puzzle, sitting above the table.* MR PERKINS *moves down* L, *sits in his chair and picks up the newspaper.* MRS PERKINS *takes up her darning*)

MRS PERKINS. 'Ow much did y' say it was worth, Pa?
MR PERKINS (*gruffly*) Never mind.
MRS PERKINS. Well, I 'ad my bit o' fun for onct.

CURTAIN

FURNITURE AND PROPERTY PLOT

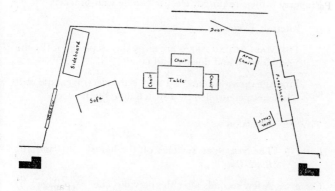

On stage: Table. *On it:* jigsaw puzzle
3 chairs
Sofa. *On it:* cushions
Armchair (*above fireplace*) *On it:* socks, mending
materials
Armchair (*below fireplace*) *On it:* newspaper
Sideboard
On mantelpiece: clock, pipe
Other fittings as required
Electric-candle wall-brackets
Blind at window

Off stage: Diamond
Revolver (STRANGER)
Revolver (ALBERT)
Whistle (ALBERT)

Personal: MR PERKINS: tobacco, matches
STRANGER: watch

LIGHTING PLOT

Property fittings required: electric-candle wall-brackets

Interior. Evening

THE MAIN ACTING AREAS are L (by the fireplace), R (by the window), C and down C and LC

THE APPARENT SOURCE OF LIGHT is the electric-candle wall brackets, controlled by a switch up C by the door

To open: Lights on

Cue 1   The STRANGER switches off the lights   (Page 16)
          Black-Out

Cue 2   A few seconds after the previous cue   (Page 16)
          The LIGHTS come up again